MW00616982

A Simple Guide
To A Happier Life

Dr. Karen McCleskey

Cover design by Richard Joule
Cover photo by Karen McCleskey
Author photo by L.J. Heflin

Palindrome Press
Atlanta

Two Important Things I'd Like to Share With You:

1. I have nothing to say that someone else hasn't already said, and in some cases, much better than I. If this is true, then you might wonder why I wrote this book. Here's the answer: my hope is very simply that something I share with you in these pages, even though you may have heard it before, will this time truly resonate within you and touch you in new ways; that you will REALLY hear and take to heart something that will lead you to even just one change that brings more happiness, joy, ease, success, and pleasure into your life.

Sometimes just the right moment occurs and we take in something that, even though we've known it for ages, becomes something wondrous as we hear it with new ears and see it with new eyes. I hope a moment like that happens for you in these pages. If it does, then writing this book will be worth every letter typed.

2. I have been influenced by and am grateful for the writing and work and thinking of the following people: (they're in alphabetical order) Marc Allen, Dr. Joan Borysenko, Dr. Viktor Frankl, Dr. John Gottman, Jack Kornfield, Rabbi Harold Kushner, HHH the Dalai Lama, Dr. Ellen Langer, Dr. Pat Love, Dr. Dean Ornish, Dr. Scott Peck, Don Miguel Ruiz, Dr. Robert Sapolsky, Dr. Martin Seligman, and Brian Tracy

For Juane

I am so happy and grateful you had the courage to imagine me and you.

Table of Contents

1.

The Wisdom of Ease:

Things Don't Always Have To Be Hard

Really? Really. It's not the norm for things to always be difficult. In fact, if everything always seems harder than it feels like it has to be, something's wrong. I'm not saying life is easy. We grow from some of life's challenges or perhaps a better term is opportunities to learn. I AM saying that life truly is supposed to be a lot less angst-filled, difficult, unmanageable, and miserable that most folks experience it to be. It's really o.k. for things to go well for you. You deserve it. You may be wondering how I can say this, given that I don't know you. I can say this without a moment's hesitation because I don't have to know you to know that you and everyone on this planet deserve the best. It's your right. You don't have to earn it. It's a gift waiting to be picked up and enjoyed. When are things hard then? When we don't accept the gift. When are things difficult? When we think it's the world and other people who are in our way and we don't recognize that we are the ones in our own way. When is life less than enjoyable? When we focus on what we don't have and forget to focus on what we do have. The key to ease is very simple: accept what is yours and always has been. There are no strings and no scorecard with this. Just remember to say Thank You.

2.

The Wisdom of the Single Step:

It's O.K. to Have

The truth is that most people are in their way a whole lot more than anyone else is. One of the best ways to be in your own way is to believe you don't deserve anything that's good. What we're talking about here is your "WIL", aka your "Worth It Level." Everybody's got one. Your Worth It Level (WIL from now on) has a tremendous amount to do with how your life goes and how you let it go. If your WIL is set low, then you probably have a life in which you feel things rarely go right. You may even sabotage things so your results prove your beliefs. I've found that way too often, people also can feel as if they need to be punished. Another issue some folks can have is the feeling that they must believe all the lies the people who mattered in their lives told them because of their own pain and problems. Keeping your WIL low will certainly help you accomplish all this. Here's my question: do you really want to keep feeling like all the truly good things in life are meant for someone else, but not for you? Everything good is meant for everyone. Everyone. NO exceptions. Everyone includes you. Believe it, accept it, act as if you believe it. Trust yourself, not someone whose only investment lies in contributing to helping you feel awful about yourself. Whatever you have to do to raise your WIL, make the commitment to doing it: Go to therapy. Go back to therapy. Read helpful books. Go to talks, workshops, retreats. Talk to people who have a high WIL. You must commit to doing whatever it takes. The goal is to get to a point where you know with every cell in your body that it's o.k. for you to have. We're not talking material things, although that can easily be part of it. What I am aiming at here is getting to a place where feeling good is expected and relished; where being happy is the norm, not the exception; where you do what you love and love what you do (and I mean this more than just about work); where you have someone who loves you and you love that person right back; where peace and contentment occur regularly, not sporadically; where your life proceeds with ease instead of agony. I am speaking of getting to a place where there are no more halves of things, only a wholeness of positive experiences. Can you imagine how wonderful your life could be if it looked like this? If you can't, that's a pretty strong sign your WIL is too low. It's never too late to raise it. Commit now.

Think about it: if things don't always have to be hard, then it follows that things going really well is o.k. The problem for many people is that they feel undeserving of things going well and ultimately feel it's not o.k. to have. So, in accordance with their belief, they don't have.

I'd like to share a personal note here. Several years ago, I was going through a particularly difficult time. A very wise, warm, and wonderful woman entered my life and she and I met weekly to talk. Not therapy. Not solving problems. Just talk. I shared. She shared. We listened to each other and to ourselves. One hot Texas afternoon we were sitting out on my deck drinking Coke out of real glass bottles and she looked over at me and said, "You know it's o.k. to have, right?"

And that's when it hit me: I had never believed it was o.k. for me to have anything. Not attention. Not love. Not people I could trust. Not the bike I really wanted. Not, Not, Not.

I'd like to tell you that an epiphany occurred and I "got it' that instant and immediately began to live my life as a person who believed having was o.k., but this is a non-fiction book. As the Buddhists like to say, "A journey of a thousand miles starts with a single step." Lynne's question to me was my "single step" on my journey toward it becoming o.k. with me for me to have. Notice I said "o.k. with me" for me to have. This is a very important, yet very subtle phrase. What it means is this: YOU are the one who decides whether to accept or decline what is already

there for you.   Now, here's my question for you:
"You know it's o.k. to have, right?"

3.

The Wisdom of Your Own Influence:

Refuse To Be Influenced By The Criticism Or The Praise Of Others

I can't begin to convey how radically different my life became when I began to incorporate this into my life. Through therapy, reading, attending workshops, being aware of when I allow others' arrows to hit me and how I choose to react to the "wound," and through just downright good old practicing, I've actually gotten pretty good at not being affected by the criticism of others. On days when I'm not really on my game with it and I've done a presentation or conducted a workshop, I put the evaluations aside until I feel able to choose to read them simply for the constructive suggestions they may provide rather than as proof positive I am a terrible teacher. But for me, dealing with praise is, as we say in the South, a whole nuther thing.

I may not be tremendously affected by criticism, but I have had to come to grips with just how affected I can be by the praise of others. Here's some insight about what makes dealing with praise a particularly slippery issue. If someone thinks you're not great or _____ (you fill in the blank with the word that works for you), then you can just about always find reasons that person is incorrect: two digit I.Q.

or unable to recognize genius when seen, for example. Now let's look at the praise part. When people think you hung the moon, since most of us respond favorably to positive things because we don't get enough of them in our lives, it becomes pretty easy to buy into the praise of others and thus lose our own sense of who we are, as decided by us. We are often strongly aware of how the hurtful comments made consciously or mindlessly by others affect or influence or change us, but just as often we are NOT aware of how we are just as strongly influenced by the praise of others.

Here's the bottom line: we think we're o.k. because someone else thinks and says we are. So what happens when someone doesn't think we're o.k.? We think we're not o.k. Now we've hit the real issue here: when we give others the power for how we feel about ourselves, we put ourselves and our feelings and our lives in the hands of someone else and we abdicate personal responsibility. The worst part of doing this is that we are no longer in charge of how we feel.

Choosing to refuse to buy into "I'm not o.k. because people think I'm not" and "I'm o.k. because people tell me I am" may be the one of the most helpful refusals you'll ever make. Learning to value what YOU think about you more than what others think about you is mostly a skill, a truly invaluable skill, but a skill nonetheless. The good news about this is that skills can be learned. Like anything you want more of, the more you do it, the more you'll do it. And, the more you refuse to be influenced by others' criticism or praise, the happier you'll find yourself. Here's the target to aim at: Live your life so that neither criticism nor praise changes you in any way that you do not consciously choose. Be o.k. with you because YOU know you're o.k., not because someone else says so. Just because someone thinks you're not o.k., refuse to be influenced by that, too. I said earlier perfection isn't the goal, but I'll share what I believe a worthy, healthy, helpful goal might be with this: do whatever it takes to know you're just fine the way you are, no matter what anyone else says, whether kind or cruel. When praise comes your way, I say make the choice to grab it, take it in, and enjoy it; do whatever it takes to relish, revel, and roll around in it and do whatever it takes NOT to deflect it. Just be sure not to let it define you.

When criticism comes your way, you've still got choices: defend, attack, be neutral, observe the whole thing non-judgmentally, smile, nod, walk away...the list of options is endless. Remember to keep in mind that the most important choice to make regarding praise and/or criticism is to be sure you use them and that you do not let them use you.

4.

The Wisdom of the Chinese Fortune Cookie:

Not Wanting To Is Reason Enough

A client asked me recently how to say NO. This led to a discussion about boundaries and various other things, including her WIL. One of her biggest concerns was how to explain her answer of NO. She shared with me that she believed that to say NO meant she had to say why she was saying NO and she couldn't figure out exactly how to explain her desired answer of

NO without making up some untruth which she strongly did not want to do. Here's where your WIL comes in. I'm not advocating rudeness, but neither am I advocating the position that in order to say NO you must justify your answer. NO needs no justification. She seemed to get my point, but at the same time, was very reticent to say the actual word NO. She then asked a very good question: "If I don't say No, what DO I say instead so that I don't end up saying Yes?" So, I made a few suggestions:

1. "I choose not to do that."

2. "I wouldn't be able to do that."

3. "I believe I'll pass on that."

4. "That doesn't work for me right now, but maybe another time" (only if this is true).

Then I encouraged her to come up with other responses on her own. She did a great job. Sometimes we just need to see how something can be done. Sometimes we just need to see that it can actually BE done, too.

Understanding that you are truly free to honor the fact that is true for you, (i.e., "I don't want to do that because I don't want to do that") and sharing that with another in a kind, yet firm manner, is absolutely one of the great markers of being an adult. It's also one of the Top Ten Things Most Guaranteed to Irritate Someone.

Why? Because all the times we said Yes, even when we wanted to say No made life easier for others. And, others are usually not too happy about losing that. This is one of the main reasons that it's so important not to explain as you move toward saying No when you really want to say No in your life. When you explain why you're saying No, it opens the door for someone to very cleverly come up with reasons why your explanation really doesn't hold water. Take a look at this example: Your neighbor asks you to pick up her kids from soccer practice when you go to pick up your daughter. You don't want to do this for a variety of very good reasons, among them being that her kids are the spawns of Satan. Rather than say NO (using one of the ways discussed previously), you say something like "I can't do that because I promised my daughter I'd take her out to eat at her favorite place after practice to celebrate her decision to become the first woman president of the United States." Then what happens? Your completely clueless, I-have-never-read-Social-Intelligence-by-Daniel-Goleman neighbor says this: "Oh, that's perfect. I just knew it would all work out. Damian and Lucifer just love that restaurant! They can go with you and then you can drop them off at the house after dinner. I should be back from shopping by then." As she pushes the button to roll up the window in your dropped-jawed face and prepares to drive away, you hear her saying to herself, "Oh, isn't it wonderful how things always work out so perfectly!" You know she's not talking about things working out wonderfully for you, right? Now what happens? The next thing you know, you're doing what you didn't want to do. Next feeling? Most likely you will find yourself feeling resentment or anger or maybe even rage, not only at the other person, but also at yourself.

Remember that some people want you to explain decisions you have made because it gives them the power to evaluate the O.K.'ness of your decisions. For these people, hearing you say "Because I just don't want to" will absolutely drive them crazy. Be strong and do not give into explaining or justifying what you do not want to do (or what you do want to do, for that matter). Once you explain, you are playing their game by their rules. Doing this will not help you feel good about yourself. Actually, it doesn't make you feel too good about the other person, either.

The all--time best Chinese fortune cookie I ever got said this:

"Never explain. Your friends don't need it and your enemies won't believe it."

Wise folks, those Chinese fortune cookie writers.

5.

The Wisdom of the Bottom Line:
Simplify

I'll bet there are hundreds of books on simplifying. That should tell you something: it's a way of living, choosing, and behaving that people are completely taken with. I also think it's one of those concepts that most folks read and read about, yet rarely put anything that they've read/learned into life-altering action. Why is this? It would seem that making things simpler would be simple, right? I mean, come on, how hard can it be to make things more simple? Actually, it can be pretty darn hard. Let's take a look at the Webster's Dictionary definition of simple:

..... *to reduce to basic essentials; make easier or reduce in complexity*

Seems easy enough, right? It is if you know what the basic essentials are. Here's where many of us get stuck: we have no idea what our basic essentials are. In fact, in order to know that, we would have to really, truly know who we are and we would have to know what we really, truly want. The answers to those questions show us who we are at our truest, most bottom-line self. They are also very scary questions to many of us. Think what would happen if you really knew who you are and what you want? Yes, think what would happen......

Personally, I think there are 2 ways to go about simplifying our lives:

1. Accept the challenge of learning who you are and what you want. As you learn more about you, you'll know what really matters to you, and knowing what really matters most to you will make it easier for you to choose what gets pared down to essentials.

OR

2. Simplify anything. Just pick something, anything, just one thing, and decide what it would take to make that thing easier, more convenient for you. As you begin to simplify things, you'll start to get a stronger, clearer sense of who you are and what you want. If # 1 seems a bit daunting right now, then go with #

2. I think what you'll find is that in choosing to simplify just one thing, you'll find yourself on the road to learning more about you at your most basic, essential self and thus, you'll eventually be simplifying your life by using # 1.

You know which one of the two is what you need to choose at this time in your life. The real choice here is simple: pick one.

6.

The Wisdom of Selection:

Choose To Use The Words "I Choose" More Often When You Speak

This is a great way to say you are taking full responsibility for what you are doing and the choices you are making. It's also one of those things that can sound better in theory than in practice. This is because it can actually be pretty scary to take responsibility for ourselves and our choices. Think of the difference between these two statements:

1. *"Oh, gee, I can't. I have to go to the company picnic."*

2. *"I choose to go to the company picnic."*

O.K., I know we both know the real choice isn't the company picnic. What's really going on here is this: "I choose to keep my job and going to the company picnic helps me do that." When we give the power over what we do to "them", we can begin to feel inadequate and small. When we take responsibility, we begin to feel more empowered and more like we have some say-so and control in our lives.

Think about the example above: do you feel a difference inside you when you HAVE to do what the company says and when YOU CHOOSE to go because you want to keep your job? It may seem like a very insignificant difference, but I assure you it's the beginning of taking control and responsibility for your life. Notice that the first statement in our example shows no personal responsibility, while the 2nd one puts the decision squarely on your shoulders. While it may feel rather uncomfortable (and it will become less uncomfortable the more you choose to do it), it's certainly the best choice for better mental health because owning your decision is a really positive and empowering thing to do. In case taking responsibility sounds really scary, then just start with one small step, with a statement that simply makes you feel good about yourself because it's empowering. Here's a good one to begin with: next time friends pressure you to go out for the evening and you don't want to, instead of saying your usual, which is probably something like "I can't. My significant other will get mad at me", try this: "I choose to stay home and have the evening to myself." You may even find that sometimes saying it only to yourself is the best choice, especially when you're first trying this out. What's important is that you say something that reflects more about what you want for yourself and less about what others want from you. By the way, you don't have to literally say "I choose...". There are several other ways to express this concept of taking responsibility. The important thing is that the concept is expressed as opposed to turning our precious personal responsibility over to someone else. Try "I choose..." for a while and experience what accepting personal responsibility at its most enlightening and empowering can feel like.

7.

The Wisdom of Holding the Reins:

Never, Ever Let Anyone Decide How You Will Act

Just because someone lays a guilt trip on you doesn't mean you have to feel guilty.

Just because someone blames you doesn't mean you have to be contrite and accept that blame.

Just because someone is angry doesn't mean you have to get angry.

Just because someone is thoughtless, rude, or downright cruel doesn't mean you have to sign up to do the same thing.

Just because someone forgot your birthday doesn't mean you have to "forget" his.

Just because someone lied about you doesn't mean you have to lie about her.

When we say things like "He just makes me so mad. That's why I spray painted his car" what's really happening is that we have handed over the reins of our emotions to someone else. When we allow others to decide how we will act, guess what else we've handed over? Yep, you guessed it: our power.

Mostly when we behave these ways, if we'll stop for just a minute, we'll see that what really happened was that we had a knee-jerk reaction. Now here's the truth about knee-jerk reactions: we believe we're in charge of them, but we're not;

other people are in charge of our knee-jerk reactions. Really. When people take that "hammer" and "tap" our knees, I vote for grabbing that little "hammer" right out of their controlling, mindless little hands. When we claim the "hammer", we claim our freedom, our choices, and most importantly, we claim our power. We don't claim our power by cutting off our "knees" or numbing our "knees". We claim our power by stopping the assault on our "knees." If you leave the "hammer" in someone else's hands, then you've handed the reins to your life over to that person and that means someone else is running your life. I originally typed ruining instead of running. I'm not so sure there's much difference between those words if the reins to your life lie in someone else's hands.

So, what's the bottom line? Just this: if you want to show your anger, show your anger. If you want to take the blame, take it. If you want to feel guilty, by all means go for it. If you don't send that birthday card, that's fine. Just make sure you are acting the way you're acting because YOU want to behave that way, not because you gave your power to someone else.

8.

The Wisdom of a Gift to Yourself:

Listen To The Advice You Give Others. Very Often It's The Advice You Need To Give Yourself.

You wouldn't believe the things I've told others about setting appropriate boundaries around areas related to self-care. The advice contained really smart, sensible, reasonable, super good things to do, too. We're not going into the number of times I didn't even get close to doing in my own life what I truly know and believe to be good for others.

Here's a simple suggestion for implementing this in a way to bring a bit more happiness into your life: really be mindful of what you tell others to do. Then step back and ask yourself this question: "Is there anything in what I just said that I need to do in my own life?" In order to get the most out of this one, really, really listen to your answer.

For example, let's say you tell a friend she needs to quit her job before she ends up in the hospital or worse. Now, step back and ask yourself "Is there any area in my life where I need to quit something?"

Sometimes it may work for you to answer the question in a very literal way: "Do I need to quit my job?" and sometimes, probably more often than not, you will gain more from answering the question a bit less literally than the example above illustrates. To get the most from the question you ask of yourself, try answering it "outside the box" and see what the answer is. If you don't seem to get a helpful answer, try answering it very literally. One way or the other, the important thing is to keep in mind that when we share what we think another ought to do, there's usually a part of ourselves in that statement. Stepping back, asking yourself "The Question", and paying very close attention to your answer just may open up a whole new world for you.

9.

The Wisdom of Saying When:

Just Because You Can Doesn't Mean You Should

The very things you are really good at may be the very things you need to stop doing. Here's a good question to use to figure out what to stop doing: "Is this serving others in a positive way and does this serve me positively as well?"

Let me share a personal example. At the age of 22, I began my entrance into the world of work as a high school English teacher. After doing this for five years, I began to feel very dissatisfied with the job and with myself.

I looked at my situation and discovered that I was actually quite good at being a high school English teacher. That didn't make me feel any better. In fact, I felt worse. Why would I quit doing something I was good at? For me, the answer was this: "Well, I may be good at it, but I'm miserable doing this."

I opted out of teaching high school. This was a hard decision to make, as most decisions involving change are. Here's the Cliff Notes version of what happened as my life evolved: I returned to school and earned my doctorate in counselor education. I have taught people to become counselors. I also do workshops and presentations, once again, I am teaching. I see clients. I see that as the ultimate "teaching". It hit me a couple of years ago that I am a teacher.

All that happened, and it was for my best, by the way, was that I needed to change the form that teaching took.

I'd like to give you a second example related to this. I have very strong verbal skills. This is a good thing to have since I teach and I counsel. Here's the not-so-good part: I have used my verbal strength to outmaneuver and overwhelm others whose verbal skills are not as strong. There's no way that changing the form here will work to serve myself or others positively. I have had to (and I continue to do so) work very hard at stopping the verbal abuse that I am quite good at creating. It can be a tough road to travel as we move toward stopping negative things, mostly because it's easy to do what we're good at. So how do we know what to stop, even though we're good at it? I believe the answer lies in the question I asked at the beginning of this chapter: "Is this serving others in a positive way and does this serve me positively as well?" If the answer is no, the behavior must go.

10.

The Wisdom of Dessert

You're Supposed To Eat Your Cake

I've heard some really idiotic things in my life, but this one really takes the cake. (pun intended).   WHY would you have cake (we're speaking metaphorically here)   that you can't eat? Can you see a picture here of someone with a wicked, toothless grin holding your absolutely favorite cake just out of your reach, but so close you can smell that cream cheese icing? Now listen to her saying something like "It's right here for you, but you can't have it." Is this not one of the most cruel things you can imagine? Sure it is.

Think for a moment about this saying: "You can't have your cake and eat it, too." Now, stop for a moment and ask yourself this: "Why not?" Then ask yourself this question: "Who made that absolutely absurd rule?" I'm going to jump in here and answer that 2nd question for you. That asinine rule was made by folks who don't believe that there's enough to go around and by some other folks who believe sadism is a reasonable lifestyle.

Personally, I believe in an abundant, overflowing with super and amazing things kind of universe; the kind of place where the very fact that there is a cake is a personal invitation to dig in. Oh, and by the way, while you're digging in, be sure you are savoring and enjoying every single bite.

Remember two things:

1. You're worth it

2. There's enough for all.

Oh, yeah, one more thing: make sure it's your absolute favorite cake!

11.

The Wisdom of Truth
or Consequences:

The Person We Lie To The Most Is Us

I'm stupid.

I'm not good enough.

I'll never be good enough.

I can't do that.

I'll do that wrong.

Nobody likes me.

Nobody loves me.

I'll never amount to anything.

I'll always be left out.

I'll never have anyone.

We don't intentionally set out to lie to ourselves. We somehow have just embraced the idea that it's better to believe you can't than to believe you can.

Sometimes the idea came from what we heard growing up. Maybe someone whose opinion we valued told us these things. Maybe their intention was to protect us, to keep us from getting our hopes up too high and being disappointed; maybe their intention was to hurt us. Maybe somewhere in our lives we learned that if we believe really positive things about ourselves then we might start thinking we're better than others, or as I heard growing up, we might get the "big head". Wherever we learned to doubt our personal worth, this lie of all lies must go. What's at stake here is our very lives.

Since life tends to work much better when there's more truth running our lives than lies, let's take a moment and look at each of the lies I began this chapter with, followed by a statement that is much, much closer to the truth:

LIE: I'm stupid.

TRUTH: I do some stupid things sometimes.

LIE: I'm not good enough.

TRUTH: There are many things I do very well.

LIE: I'll never be good enough.

TRUTH: I am already good enough.

LIE: I can't do that.

TRUTH: I can't do that yet, but I will choose to learn to.

LIE: I'll do that wrong.

TRUTH: I might do it wrong, but I won't know until I try. If it turns out that I do it wrong, I will choose to try again.

LIE: Nobody likes me.

TRUTH: Somebody likes me, but I don't like them so they don't count.

LIE: Nobody loves me.

TRUTH: I want to be loved a certain way. No one loves me in the only way I am open to receiving love.

LIE: I'll never amount to anything.

TRUTH: I don't know this yet. The odds are astronomically in my favor that I will do something positive with my life.

LIE: I'll always be left out.

TRUTH: I may feel left out now and I will do whatever it takes for me to learn how I can be with others in a healthy and positive way.

LIE: I'll never have anyone.

TRUTH: I know there's a lid for every pot and that includes me. Just because I don't have my lid right now doesn't mean I never will.

LIE: I lie to myself.

TRUTH: I know this isn't in my best interest and I choose to work on telling myself my truth. I trust that I can do this and I trust me.

12.

The Wisdom of Good Fences:

Say No To More Work

First, you've got to be able to say NO. Why NO to more work? Because work always expands to fit the time you have open. Do you really want more work? Or do you, like most people, want more time to spend with people you care about and more time to spend with yourself, enjoying life and all the wondrous things it has to offer?

Let's take a minute and see if we can figure why people tend to say Yes to more work. Here's a thought: maybe it's because fear is at the root of this.

Before I proceed with this, I want to be clear that if you really want to say Yes to more work, then you may want to skip this chapter and go to the next one. Saying No to more work isn't for everyone, although in my personal opinion, everyone should say No to more work for a variety of exceptionally good reasons we'll talk about soon. But for now, let's go back to fear. What would lead a perfectly rational person to be afraid to say No to more work? In no particular order, here are some of the most common answers:

-I could lose my job.

-I could lose my customers.

-"They" will think I'm not a team player.

-I won't get promoted (or a raise or a better parking space).

-I need the money. (I'm afraid of having less money).

-If I'm not working, what will I do?

These are just a few of the fears we all face when considering saying No to more work. As you can see, some of them have to do with letting go of what others think of us. Some of them have to do with wants or preferences we may need to reconsider the importance of. The last one has to do with fear of being alone with yourself. It may even have to do with fear of change.

Work does provide many people with an "acceptable" excuse for not doing things: "I'd love to _____, but I've got so much work to do." This works nicely when we use it for things we really don't want to do; however, it really doesn't serve us well at all when it's the truth and it interferes with things we really want to do.

Earlier I mentioned that there are some very good reasons to say No to more work. In a nutshell, here they are:

1. The U.S. has surpassed Japan in the death rate from overwork.

Is your job worth your life?

2. Career research has shown us that the best way to do a really good work at your job is to have scheduled breaks away from the job.

It's hard to schedule and take a break when you say Yes to more work.

3. When you choose to say No to more work, once you get by any fear that this brings up, you may find yourself feeling empowered and more in control of your life.

4. Americans work the longest hours among industrialized nations.

5. Half of white-collar workers log fifty or more hours a week working.

6. 42% of Americans are working more hours now than five years ago.

Research from social psychologists shows us that people who feel empowered and more in control of their lives tend to be happier and to live longer. I could go on and on with this, but instead I'd like to recommend a wonderful book titled <u>Your Money or Your Life</u> by Joe Dominguez and Vicky Robin.

Bottom line with this chapter? Say No when you want to say No. Saying NO to more work may be scary because it's something we've never done before. If you can't or don't know how to or are afraid to, then reach out for help. It could save your life.

Consider this wonderful and challenging quote by Aldous Huxley: "They intoxicate themselves with work so they won't see who they really are." Are you afraid that not having every moment filled with work will show you things about yourself that you'd rather not see?

13.

The Wisdom of Less:

Do 1 Thing At A Time

Multi-tasking isn't normal. It's the bane of a normal person's existence. Please keep in mind that the definition of bane is "something causing misery or death", according to the Princeton Dictionary. Let's tie the first two sentences together. How about something like this: Multi-task and Die. That has the sound of a great bumper sticker. It also has the sound of truth. According to recent research on the brain, multi-tasking is one of the most destructive things we can do to it. If hurting your brain doesn't grab your attention, how about hurting your body? Ever wondered why so many states have passed laws that you can't drive and be on your cell phone at the same time? There's another issue with multi-tasking. Since we've looked at the definition of bane, let's continue expanding our vocabularies for the day we get on Jeopardy and look at some definitions of mindful. Attentive, conscientious, aware are some of the words that show up as synonymous with mindful. Mindful learning, mindful lovemaking, mindful relationships, mindful business practices, mindful parenting, ... you name it. We can choose anything and make a decision to be more mindful or if you prefer, more aware or more attentive or more conscientious, of it. Think of it as being awake at the wheel of whatever you're doing instead of having no idea what you're doing and in some cases, no memory of what you did. I've heard so many people say that if they didn't multi-task, they wouldn't never get anything done. I think what might be more accurate is that if they didn't multi-task, they would get more things done with greater ease and competence, and with much less frustration.

So why one thing at a time? Because one thing at a time allows for focus, which adds to and heightens the pleasure, the joy, and the exquisite happiness that so many things bring to our lives. Because one thing at a time brings an embrace of life's experiences rather than an avoidance of them.

14.

The Wisdom of Flexibility:

It's Really OK To Change Your Mind

Why in the world would we not change our minds if we got better information? Or if we got better insight into ourselves and what we want?

The people who say bad things about people who change their minds are usually the ones who are inconvenienced by the mind change someone has.

If you think that changing your mind is about being selfish, let me assure you it's not.

Consider that, for the most part, things that are in your best interest are usually in others' best interests, too. They just might not be able to see this at the time.

I believe there are really only two things to look at when considering changing your mind:

1. Am I being frivolous or capricious? In other words, am I acting without being mindful? (if you're stopping to ask yourself this question, then the odds are that the answer is No.)

2. Will changing my mind be helpful to me and serve me in a positive way?

If the answer to the first question is No and the answer to the second question is Yes, then changing your mind just might be the best change you make today.

15.

The Wisdom of Priorities:

Choose You

I once said to a client that every time she chose another child to help, she did not choose her own children. Fortunately, she took this well.

Every time we say Yes to someone else when we don't want to, we say NO to ourselves and to those who love us. I really believe you can make about as much money as you set your mind to make, but there's only so much time. Once it's spent, you don't make more and you can't get it back. What does this have to do with this chapter? Everything. You either choose you or you choose others. Please know that I am not saying you should always choose you. There are times that choosing others is the best, right, most sensible and reasonable choice to make. My focus on this is to make the point that always choosing others is harmful to you and those who love you. Committed love relationships end because of this. Children feel discounted and unvalued because of this. You may find yourself feeling spread too thin and experiencing mental and physical exhaustion. It takes a lot of energy to put everyone else's needs before your own. Folks with the misleading (sounds like a compliment, but trust me, it's not) label of "people pleasers" seem to have the most trouble with making a choice to choose themselves. This is a snapshot of what runs through their minds: "Let me see here. I can choose to do/be/give what others want even if doing so isn't in my best interest or I can choose me. Well, I better choose them. After all, what right do I have to put my needs/wants/preferences anywhere on the list?

Besides, if I don't please others by complying or accommodating, they won't like me anymore." This is one of the most harmful and dangerous ways we hurt ourselves. What's so incredibly ironic is that we believe that it's the most helpful thing we can do. I have a note posted to my desk. It says this: I refuse to put others first when doing so comes at the expense of myself. Sounds pretty radical, doesn't it? Actually, for many people it is a radical choice to put themselves first, to choose themselves. Only when we believe we matter, too, and we make choices that attest to that belief will we really be helpful to others, and ultimately ourselves.

16.

The Wisdom of What's Between Do and Don't:

Ignore Yoda. It's Really O.K. To Try

It's a classic movie scene: the young Jedi (Luke) is struggling and not doing very well. His wise mentor (Yoda) continues to encourage him. Finally, the young Jedi says "I'll try" to which Yoda says "Do not try. Either do or not do." I know it's dangerous to suggest that something Yoda says should be ignored, but I'm feeling brave today. Here's why I'm asking that we reconsider Yoda's advice: because trying counts. It means giving something your best effort, even if it doesn't succeed. If you think about it, trying is doing. Maybe Yoda was splitting hairs on the word and maybe I am, too.

And, maybe those hairs need to be split. How many times have you said what Luke said? How many times have you said with a determined, positive attitude, "I'll try" only to have it shot down by someone who doesn't get that your willingness to try is a really big deal and should be fully, completely supported? Here's a good come-back to those folks: "Trying IS doing."

Trying isn't a guarantee that success will follow, but success can't follow without the attempt to TRY. Make a commitment to give yourself and others support and encouragement when an "I'll TRY" comment is made. It may seem like a small thing, but I believe you'll find it will make a big difference when you give yourself permission to TRY. TRY, not succeed and not fail, just TRY.

17.

The Wisdom of Sharing:

Delegate

If you're wondering why Delegate is a chapter, please take another look at the title of this book. When we learn to let others do something, too, (aka delegate), that's a huge step toward having a happier life. Delegating can free up precious time for you to have to spend with people you love, doing things you love to do. For those people we delegate to, there can be a wonderful feeling of being trusted with responsibility.

Being able to delegate is truly the mark of a leader's leader. While I'm using a word like "leader", please know that I am talking about more than a work or business setting. Those are typically the arenas where 'delegate' is used most, but delegating can help in all relationships because delegating says this about the person delegating: "I'm not afraid to share the power. I'm not afraid to trust that you can do something just as well as I can, maybe even better. I'm not afraid."

Just think about how different so many areas of our lives would be if we let go of the fear of letting others have appropriate responsibilities.

This one action will strengthen your primary love relationship, your relationship with friends, with your children, and maybe even your family if for no other reason than the person feels honored to have such trust placed on her or him.

I once heard Dr. Pat Love say that if you're always the helper and never the helpee, that you are actually denying someone a chance to feel how good it feels to help; that always being the helper is really a selfish thing to do.

One of my strongest personal beliefs is to make as many situations as possible be win-win. I think giving up whatever keeps us stuck in fear about accepting or asking for help is also what can lead to win-win situations.

There's just one more thing I would like to add about delegating. When you decide to call on your courage and delegate, please, please, please don't criticize if what you delegated isn't done perfectly. Just keep in mind that just as delegating is a new behavior for you, being delegated to is new behavior for the person you chose to trust by delegating to her or him.

18.

The Wisdom of Learning:

Never Let Suffering Be Your Only Teacher

No pain, no gain is one of the most destructive comments I've ever heard. It implies that the only way to achieve or accomplish something is through misery.

People move toward pleasure and they move away from pain. As Dr. Joan Borysenko says: "Do what you will, not what you won't." She is so right because if you won't do whatever it is, that means you won't do anything at all.

Ask yourself: how do I learn?

Your answer to this question will tell you much about who you are.

For example, many of us tend to learn by the 2 x 4 method: we have to get hit over the head with one to wake up and see what we need to change or do differently.

Unfortunately, this model has been the only one many people know about. Is there an alternative? I believe the answer is YES and here it is: pay attention to what brings you joy and let it be o.k. to learn just as much from what you like as you do from what you don't like. Never, ever buy into "Push through the pain." Not only is this stupid advice, but it is potentially harmful as well. Keep in mind that just because you choose not to "push through the pain" doesn't mean you don't feel pain or that you avoid feeling pain. It simply means that you are smart enough to know when enough is enough.

As a therapist, I've seen   people learn and cry tears of joy as often as learning and shedding tears of regret and frustration.

Yes, pain and suffering can teach you and there is certainly a place and time for learning in that way. And, we must be mindful of the truth that the joyous lessons we learn are equally valuable.

19.

The Wisdom of Stopping
and Starting:

*Stop Spending Time Doing Things That Are Not
In Your Best Interest So You'll Have Time For
The Things That Are In Your Best Interest*

How do you know what's in your best interest?

You'll feel joy, a kind of peaceful easiness, and something like a mellow kind of calmness. Thoughts like "I hate this" will not occur to you.

Whatever is in your best interest will feel "right". If this is a rare feeling for you it may be that you might not recognize it right off the bat. In fact, for some, feeling the above feelings may actually feel uncomfortable because they are not used to feeling anything joyful. Time flies; you smile more, you have more patience, you feel more like who you were created to be.

20.

The Wisdom of Fear:

Remember That Fear Is Generally More About The Future Than The Present

Make a list of everything you can think of that you're afraid of.

Now go through your list and put a ✓ by everything that has actually happened. You may be surprised by how few things you've been living in fear of have actually happened.

I am not saying going through life completely and totally with absolutely no fear is the way to go. That attitude is simply stupid and is a good way to end up hurt or dead. It's just that it is one thing to pay fear its due respect; it's another to hand your life over to fear and let it rule your life. True confession time: I have snake-aphobia. Even just typing that word sent a chill through me. I'm sure that's not the correct word, but I don't want to look it up because there might be a picture of one of them (you know...)

While hiking in the mountains of New Mexico a few years ago, I came upon a sign that said this:

"Please stay on the path and respect the rattlesnake's privacy." After a brief moment wondering if the pain in my chest was the first sign of an impending heart attack, I actually thought about the real meaning of the sign. The sign didn't say "Watch out for all the rattlesnakes because at their annual convention they voted to hunt you and only you down to the very ends of the earth in order to capture you and sink millions of deadly fangs into you and then form a circle around you while the rattling of their tails grows ever more deafeningly loud until you die a long, horrible, fear filled death." The true intention of the sign was simply a reminder to be aware that the earth is shared by all of us and that the moral thing to do is to be aware that privacy should be respected. After all, I wouldn't want someone invading my privacy by tromping through my home with no regard for the fact that I, too, live here.

While my new insight didn't cure me of my phobia, it did create a sense of empathy for the reptiles. I basically then saw the sign as saying something more along the lines of "We won't bother you if you don't bother us."

Think about this: by simply watching where I was walking, not sticking my hands into dark, hidden places, and staying on the path, I could still enjoy hiking without allowing my irrational fear to keep me at home spending huge amounts of money on the Home Shopping Network. My fear was truly based on what I perceived the future to hold rather than what has actually transpired in my life.

Fear has a place in our lives. It protects us, gives us hints at dangerous things, and in many cases, causes us to stop and think before we act.

Having an appropriate place in our lives, however, is very different than surrendering our lives to fear and allowing it to run our lives.

It seems to me that a life lived from a fear base isn't much of a life.

21.

The Wisdom of Necessities:

Be Kinder Than Is Necessary

Why? Isn't the old adage "An eye for an eye"? (someone wisely said that doing that would leave everyone blind and that's not very appealing.)

I have no idea who to credit for the following story. If it's yours, please don't sue me. Just let me know and I will credit you appropriately in the 2nd edition.

A young man went to Japan to study the martial arts. He was making wonderful progress and had begun to feel confident about his skills. One day, he was riding home from his lesson on the train. The train made a stop and a dirty, stinky, scary-looking, half-mad man (who had obviously been drinking too much sake) boarded. The look in his eyes said he was looking for trouble. After boarding, he grabbed a man and threw him out of his seat, although he himself didn't take the seat. He yelled obscenities at a frightened looking 80 year old. The young martial arts hero was taking all this in and decided if the man did one more aggressive thing, he would step in and use his new found martial arts moves to render the man unconscious, thus making the train safe once again. As expected, the man began another aggressive move, but before the young martial arts fellow could step in, a very old, very small man stood up and walked over to the troublemaker. Now the young man thought he would have to rescue two people. He was again getting geared up to save one and all, but then the old man began talking to the man. He spoke quietly and kindly and with an obvious interest in the man. The man began his belligerent behavior again, but the old man interrupted and mentioned the bottle of sake, saying how much he too, liked sake. The troubled man raised his arm, the sake bottle in his hand. but before he completed his move, the old man leaned up on his tip-toes and gently took the bottle from the man. He marveled at the brand of sake, then returned the bottle to the man. He asked the man what kind of job he had that he could afford such wonderful sake. The troubled man seemed confused, but after a few seconds he replied, "I am an engineer for one of the airlines." "Oh, my," said the little old man. "What a wonderful, exciting job!"

The troubled man looked down, ashamed, and said it had been a wonderful job, but that he had just lost his job.

By this time, the old man motioned for the man to sit down by him and tell him what happened. To the amazement of all on the train, the man sat where the old man pointed. He once again held up his bottle of sake, but the old man didn't flinch. He seemed to know he was in no danger. "You see this sake?" yelled the man. The old man said soothingly that yes, he did indeed see the sake, adding that having a drink of sake with his wife when he got home was one of the things he most looked forward to. At this, the man began sobbing uncontrollably with his head bowed and his whole body shaking. The old man put his hand on the man's shoulder and asked him what was making him so utterly sad. After a very long in breath, the man said, "I, too, loved having a drink with my wife when I would get home from work. But now there is no work." He paused, turned and looked the old man squarely in the eyes and said, "And now there is no wife either. She died a week ago." The man broke down once again. The old man slowly and gently pulled the man so that his head was in the old man's lap, stroking the man's head. As the young martial arts hero got off at his stop, he looked once again at the two men. He realized the angry man who got on the train earlier was really a man whose heart was broken into a million pieces. He caught the eye of the old man as he stepped off; their eyes locked for the ever so slightest second, then both men acknowledged each other with a slight nod of the head.

As he walked to his home, the young man gave thanks for the old man and asked that he, too, could someday be so wise.

We all have a choice in every moment: we can be the young man with physical skills to protect others or we can be the old man with the wisdom to protect and love others.

I ask that we each make a solemn vow right now to be kinder that might seem necessary.

22.

The Wisdom of the Extended Hand:

Take The Help That's Offered
(thanks to Dr. Randy Pausch for this one)

John Wayne. Yep, little readers, that's the answer to why we are so reluctant to accept help. And we're just talking about accepting help that someone else offers. God forbid that we actually ASK someone to help. Nope, that little issue is another book entirely.

Mutual dependence, being able to count on someone is a very healthy thing. Other people feel good when they get to help and not to let them actually deprives them of feeling good. (No pressure, just facts to ponder)

Think about how good you feel when you get to help someone. Well, how about we share that by letting others help.

Think about when you need help.

Now think about when someone has come along, and you declined the assistance. Any thoughts about why? Good. Now stop reading and write them down. Or write them in the margins of this book, although that will bring down the re-sale value, but hey, some things are more important than money, right?

Don't take help that really won't help you, meaning don't accept help simply because you don't know how to say No, thank you. I'm talking about how we don't accept help because we've been brainwashed to believe that if we can't do it ourselves, we are not good or smart or whatever enough.

We've been brainwashed to believe we should be able to do it all ourselves.

The Duke's been gone a long time, but I can't help but believe he would not care for how we have perverted asking for help. He might ask us to think of asking for help as a strength, not a weakness.

Note From Karen:

First, thank you so much for taking time to read my book. It is truly my most sincere hope that you found the material helpful.

If you have a moment to share your thoughts about and experience of <u>A Simple Guide</u>..., I would really love to hear from you. (It will provide me with more ways to practice # 3!)

Here are ways to reach me:

Snail Mail: Dr. Karen McCleskey
2107 N. Decatur Rd., # 185
Decatur, GA 30033

E-mail: karen@karenmccleskey.com
karenmccleskey@comcast.net

Text: 404-754-2677

Other books by the author:

Creating a Love That Lasts

Attachment: What It Is, How To Do It, and Why It Matters So Much

MAPP: A Manual for Success in Private Practice

CAPP: A Manual for Creating Professional Presentations

Please take a moment to visit Karen's websites:

www.karenmccleskey.com
www.ASGTAHL.com
www.counselorsconnecting.com
www.smartpartnering.com
www.MAPPSUCCESS.com
www.CAPPSTERS.com
www.beauandbowzer.com